MW00965614

THE UNDERWATER TYPEWRITER

Marc Zegans

The Underwater Typewriter by Marc Zegans

ISBN-10: 1938349296
ISBN-13: 978-1-938349-29-4
Library of Congress Control Number: 2015942439

Copyright © 2015 Marc Zegans

This work is licensed under the Creative Commons Attribution-NonCommercial-NoDerivatives 4.0 International License. To view a copy of this license, visit http://creativecommons.org/licenses/by-nc-nd/4.0/.

An earlier version of "First Watch" appeared in *Ibbetson Street 34*, November 2013
"ephemere" first appeared in Lyrical, *The Somerville News*, April 16, 2014
An earlier version of "Anacoluthon" appeared in *The Wick*, Summer/Fall 2010
"requiem for a spoken word" first appeared in Lyrical, *The Somerville News*, July 24, 2013
"A Hipster Retires" first appeared in *Boston Small Press and Poetry Scene*, January 9, 2012
"Somerville" first appeared in Lyrical, *The Somerville Times*, January 18, 2012

Layout and Book Design by Mark Givens

First Pelekinesis Printing 2015

For information:
Pelekinesis, 112 Harvard Ave #65, Claremont, CA 91711 USA

www.pelekinesis.com

The Underwater Typewriter

Marc Zegans

For Max and for Meri

The Underwater Typewriter

Marc Zegans

Contents

Clouding

Her eyes, turbulent as milk
mixing black tea, barely asking
for a promise that will not be given,
wash and shudder in dream and sorrow.

Hope against truth quivers her copper irises
and I doubt for a moment my place in all this,
but then I remember, and know that I am at fault.

first watch

I dreamed you just now, exploring the mossed
wreckage of an ancient wooden ship
raised up a thousand feet or more
by groaning winch, and chains stained at each link
the wood of compression ribbing gouged hull
such density between the ring-lines

bowed and jointed, sealed by wood pitch, traceless
resolved by gaps to form unfitted
"A ship still? Is the bell still ringing watch?"
I know then that you will take my hand
run your fingers long its aging creases
knowing too well the sound of eight bells,

and scan its badly stuttered lines, finding
charted there the route of second passage.

suspension

your eyes, jade tonight
were slate this morning
direct from Rajasthan
stunned time, fixing flame

sparks a thousand times
between then and now
as you gave time back
its course, gold in azure

salt

we talked in dust
climbed the saw-cut
sat cross-legged
on stumps, facing
flash irises

above the hum
our fossil tree
a telling post
a fading place
an envelope

(I had no guard)
the only spot
I had no eye
for tail draggers
and succubi

your pull marin
a foretelling
of breton chop
the day I hauled
from blooded sea

her puking frame
shivering blue
on the gunnel
her draining leg
gashed hip to knee

sheet in my teeth
making for shore
your pull marin
never salted
in sun always

on the foredeck

i remember
you safe above
taking me up
to be untouched

an un-writing
as I un-wrote
her certain death
learning from you
the hold of grace.

P(un)k Poets: Too Fucked to Drink

At round end of no corner bar
Me and Ripper backs to stage
Grab filthy glasses in plastic
Polynesia, tilt bottom shelf

Exhale and converse.

Behind us, shirtless, gobbed
in maggot wriggle, Jello
admonishes black and stinking
pogo crowd to be Republican

Never thinking

that one year hence, kill the poor
will find happy embrace in red
states more scared of welfare
than war, and tuck sunny Ron

In Washington

where healthy school lunch
is six french fries
and ketchup, not rotting
is a vegetable.

I remember the cop cars
burning that Dan White
night, but more I remember
the sidewalk outside Twin

Peaks, corner of Market

Home to freaks, long before
San Francisco urban chic
and ENG, new to me
pushing and shoving

Starting a riot.

That's the story never told
about that San Francisco
But I saw the news crews
Spiking rage, as spilt Milk

Mayor of Castro

and de-centered Moscone
were shoved aside, TV slap
at gay pride, and twinkie
excuse, kernel of conservative
human rights, now running

thirty years in low-tax CA
waiting for the day
when limited Government
would metastasize.

II

Short eyes
has become
short lines
frictionless
the times
demand
Williams
not Whitman

a pressure
constant
hard clash
words short
text words
un-vowel
no space
for air

fk u

the times
demand
Williams
not Whitman

Shall we
give way

capitu-late
or do it early.

The times
demand
Williams
not Whitman

Spondee on
Spondee

consonant
diamonds
bent light
facet play

a flash

The times
demand
Williams
not Whitman

III

Is it our work now to surrender long lines, to Howl no more, clicking
          faster, clicking faster, clicking faster, till letters
are too much, too much information to see; till we pixel click our
          way in a vaster, faster space of small screens isolated
but accessible? Is it our work now to surrender long lines, to turn
          the dirt on Allen's grave, to give less and less and send
more and more and more? Is it time to drop the analogue growl of
          John Lee singing Boom, Boom, Boom, Boom, Howl, Howl,
Howl, Howl, a different kind of howl, a wolf moanin' at midnight?
          Is it time to gate that mouth, to muzzle the grit, to join
the raft of bits? Is it time? Is it time? Is it time? Is this any more a
          question? Can time demand? Can there be a moment
on a virtual raft? "A moment?" Not moments! Not any moment!
          "A moment?" A moment to move, time justified?

          "Nooooooo!" Howls the clown prince.
          In a world without foundation, not even time
          not even these times, not even this moment
          can announce anything. The times don't
          give us an historical curl. We cannot
          surf anymore to shore on "the times."
          This time, it is on us. The times demand
          nothing, but what will we demand of ourselves?

In Turns

the savage detector raised a fragment of glass,
green and refractive at the fracture line,
to the side of his forearm, and drew it
down along the bone in calligraphic

sweep, circling the knob on his wrist as if
it were a traffic roundabout, spitting
sparkling cars from its pinwheel teeth
the evanescent light of abrasion

traveling happy into night's swallow
knowing that more hearts were meant to follow
the expulsive force of a turning wheel
powered by a small boy soon grown tired

thumb reddened by the effort, and magic
waning as sparks simply became more sparks
to a popcorn filled, cotton candy sick child
walking slowly across steaming asphalt

to his family's dirty vinyl seated car,
inside of which he would ride home too tired
for sleep, the plastic pinwheel neglected
but not abandoned by achy fingers

from which it dangled for the full ride.
the savage detector drew now the glass
along the depression west of his thumb
as the sleepy child sliding into bed

crooked his arm, spun the wheel a final time
sending sparks deep into the green glass night.

The Reunion of Darkness

Imagine two perfect absences
separated by interval
un-reckoned by the cycles of light.

Imagine a longing distance
the separation of gravities
aching...aching, aching to combine.

Imagine a life of no moments
an un-heating painful awareness.
Would this life without markers

have a sensation akin to slowness
or is that a layering of time's
perspective on formless yearning?

II

The darknesses relinquished the ache
blending gravities without ripple
conscious of each other's density

groundless, lightless conversation
will-less and without desire
playing together these darknesses.

Imagine the quiet of no hurt
when the silent call is abandoned
by the darknesses interleaving.

Woodshed

    I want

to
    make   pattern
               with words

            a sketch
in type

      for black
         and red

        and blinking

         yellow lights

                 along Broadway

that might

come

      to life

        in ways

           the painter

                                        freezes in

section.

                 A diagram

                         of Pete

                                 Johnson

        keys

                 pouring

                         in straight eights

                                                 from street lights

foresees

a bid
                to step

                         from mind

                                 to music

or call

        from dust

                 a stepper's ball.

                                        To make

                        this graph

                                        across

                    the page
to merge

                    desire

                        and score

    is to be

            a player.

                                        In the days

                        of seanchaí

poets were

            players.

        Today

            too often

                    we forget

too much

        concerned

with tongue

        governing;

        too little

            pleased

                with tips

        to lips!

Of Irish Descent

I caught your hair
between my fingers

and waited, till the sun
went down, to move

in gradual curve
along your soft neck

tracing the blackened
inner curl of waves

that ran higher
on the shore

as measured
by our feet

sand pulling
deep beneath

than when our faces
blistered in the light.

I took you then
to our fragile home

of interlude, and waves
crashing sandstone

knowing the tide would ease
your troubled sleep

but now your fair
Irish skin was alive

peeking from the folds
of my high bed

your hair turning silky
as we kissed

your seal coat buried
on distant shore

reminder
of coming turn to sea

when I, a Rumanian
landsman, would stare

over swell, and beds
of kelp, wondering

if once more you
would rise for me.

Salvage

On the third wreck the damage is greater.
Can it be said to have integrity
sufficient to warrant a ship's name
when element and corroded piece lie

wedged, current carried, sanded, scattered
in rift and rise, ripple and rip on this
unsounded ocean floor; a place without
bearing, weight uncarried, so much lighter

destination lost with the foregone hull?
This stuff we bring up has no narrative.
We construct a context of time and place
imagining which lives, with what ends

heaved with the waves of a ship unfound.
Who built it and why? What were their hands like?
As we bring these scraps to surface, are we
engaged in speculative reconstruction?

Collage, perhaps deluded? It's not clear.
Yet we haul and fondle worn bits, gauging
texture and mass, function and fit, and loss
holes and breakage, sometimes signifying.

II

On the second wreck, the ship's divided.
We see the bifurcated hull as one.
This cruel and unnatural forking begs
flotation bags, salvage boat standing by

a ride to dry dock, scuppers emptying
hoards of men to bring this named vessel
forward into commemorative glory
rust sanded, rifts repaired with perfect plates

black paint with deeper gloss and more correct
than original ever could have been
a present construction of living past
coming to life only when it breaks down

in small ways that invite and find repair
under hands of men, who scrape, paint and weld
refusing salt's rust, looking aft then fore
to the bow's clean cut, water divided.

III

On the first wreck there's a fiberglass gash.
We see translucent threads in the shallows
where a dumb day sailor on a rental
ran her into reef while drinking too much beer.

The wounded boat waves, sorry and hollow
"I'm innocent, I didn't ask for this.
I was ever alert, scanning the floor.
It didn't matter. They didn't listen."

We hoist the boat, *Subtle Wink*, easily
tow her home past goo goo rubberneckers.
Everyone knows the story, gossiping
as we chug into harbor, nothing fixed.

Finely

You tore my resting heart from its pillow
offered it, then, beating, to the sun gods
the remaining blood spattering your face
my brain, filled with useless knowledge, dying

quickly. the old body following suit
I was all heart now, held high in your hand
perfect to the light, the breeze, goose-bumping
elegant muscle too long held in check

unleashing now a profusion of roots
thirsty fibers driving through topsoil
boring through chalk, deep into wet gravel
tasting iron and salt, mineral tracings

carried quick from mountains far to the North
feeding masses of fast tendrils dancing
cross your skin in thigmotropic consort
with the curve of your hand, your arm, your cheek

your lips, your throat, your breast, a joyful gasp
as new life finely touches you inside.

Poems for the Ego

the ego's alias
pressed green moroccan hash
into a small brass bowl
in the church row alley
by the cemetery
the night the rainbow closed

he lit it with a Bic
solemnly passed it round
then showed the girls the patch
of red velvet he'd cut
so that he'd always have
a piece of the rainbow.

        II

the ego's alias wore unstructured
on the top floor of Danceteria
spoke with a girl in a clear plastic dress
who kept spilling her Curaçao cocktail
on the front-zippered furniture cover
that signaled, "look but don't touch," the same way
the living room couches teased him in Queens
daring him endlessly to put his hand
beneath the protection, soiling fabric
fingers caressing industrial silk.

        III

the ego's alias unzipped
her sensible blue corporate skirt
unbuttoned her silk corporate blouse
kicked her two inch heel corporate pumps
in small arcs across the parquet tiles
glued to the concrete floor
of her corporate Stuy-town 1-bed
unhooked her tiny corporate bra

looked at the ugly red puckers
marking her corporate white torso
rolled down her corporate pantyhose
ran fingers through her sweaty pubes
ate three spoonfuls of cottage cheese
topped with Gristedes blueberries
drank tap water from the shower
running through her corporate blond hair

dried herself with a discount towel
lay down on her corporate futon
chinese silk lavender pillow
over her computer stressed eyes
her tiny bones lost in the quilts
her body shaking into sleep
broken by her ringing alarm
pulling on now her plastic dress.

IV

the ego's alias, sloppy drunk
remembering the people he'd shot
in the line of duty as a cop
sat on the floor, head banging the wall
as he argued with Boston's finest
that he was an Oklahoma cop
that the party had to go on
that the music could hardly be heard
by the neighbors who had never complained.

V

the ego's alias reached
arm toward acoustic ceiling
then swooned on the beer-stained couch
classical acting training
on display in a New York

walk-up, brick wall, track-lighting
drawing no one's attention.

VI

the ego's alias smoked Chesterfields
wore clear glass in genuine horn-rimmed frames
purchased cashmere top-coats at Paul Stuart
wore pink button-down shirts from Brooks Brothers
boring, thick four-in-hand ties from J. Press
distinguished cap toes from Allen Edmonds
wearily pined for John Lobb oxfords
blew managing partners in bathrooms
and had needle tracks between his toes.

Sunken Contents

In the moment of fall
the slur, the cut, the jibe,
mast snapping, decapitating,
wind driven swing of the boom,
roll over—you dropping too fast,
too deep for them to touch, much
less bring you level. Proclaimed Mingus
you can't be brought low when you are beneath
the underdog, and falling fast from that subjugated
position, humiliation is an indulgent luxury, consumed
by those who imagine that loss of position carries meaning
to the death. It is a meme thing that, a transmitted misreading
of self, soul and scripture that causes endless harm, inviting as it does
all manner of violent substitute for discourse. And that is the virtue of the drop.
When you fall fast and hard, your guts having long exited your mouth, your pain
a curiosity to those who watch you writhe, *and critical comment on some embarrassing*
position, from which you long departed, arriving perhaps through no fault of your own—chuff—
at a new, soon passed, lower place, its station sign black on white streaking by, as you descend
further still, no longer wondering when you will get off the train, but only will it slow down long enough
for you to see something of the landscape in clear focus—you pine for unblurred edges, for the considered
moment, a longing satisfied fleetingly if you are lucky, and you rarely are, or so you think, at such moments
doesn't really affect you. And so the nasty introject is not so much silenced as muffled by a deepening pool
of water that scatters light at its surface, bends it at the point of penetration, and absorbs it on the descent.

Those who have not taken the fall, imagine that when you hit "rock bottom," you will be shattered utterly.
You like Humpty will be blown to bits, and them sorry-assed, domesticated minions who can't or won't
think for themselves will be powerless to help you, as if it were them you'd be turning to in the first place.
Yes the bottom is solid, but you reach it slow, your relative buoyancy rises as you plumb the depths, and
 you bounce along the bottom as an astronaut walks the moon, light on your feet, but clumsy. Unlike the rising
astronaut's vacuum ballet, you are dancing in heavy liquid, you feel the compression at every turn.
If you remain, you will fold in, diminish, curl and deflate until you have become a hard point, a grain of sand,
visible, but unremarkable in every aspect, and there, washed by tide you will slowly and eternally recede.

We who arrive at this place are not broken, but we can barely move, and we can barely see. We cannot
speak, for to open our mouths would be to drown. In our wiser and more hopeful moments we simply
direct our eyes to where the light seems brightest and move as best we can in that direction,
rising slowly, stripping away the weights that have dragged us down, eschewing
the deadly density of the lower regions, pulling toward the surface slowly.
It is on the ascent that we have time to consider the landscape,
and consider it we must, or we will rise too fast, finding
ourselves crippled at the surface by our own blood
gasses. It is in the ascent that we learn
what lay beneath us, and how far
we had yet to come, before
we could speak truth,
our truth, in clear
and ringing
voice.

Laundry and Grief

Her darling light quiet now, receding
too dim for shadow; her open eyes
un-puddled by grief, light on nothing
as her dust flicked lashes, un-twitched
wait ready.

Fall River Girl

In white wintered light she rose,
drawing swift from drowsy sheets
before sun broke the silver scrim
stretched sky to snow, revealing
and masking Cambridge Common

and she, bringing muted sterling
glow to cello curve of back at edge
obscuring day's detail, leaving only
rolling contour for my weary rods

At open door, on beveled threshold
her foot found rise, and she, lover
of heels and wearing none, pressed
toes to wood, lifting arch, pivoting
pulling me by line of sight, up from sand
of night, to her flowing edge, where we held

drawing

She'd come with toes painted purpler than plums
Darker than eggplant, and deep in the blues
I could sense the red current underneath
A tidal flow of electricity

Most women's painted toes shout, "Look at me!
See how red I am! See how gold! How pink!
how pearlescently lustrous I can be!"
As if every part must be a sign-post

A ballyhoo for that which isn't there
She'd come quieter, drawing my hand

Lotería

Will you bring me the gift of luck
tonight, my love? Or press in my hand
a wrinkled cardboard icon, corners
frayed, *el paraguas*, for the rain

or perhaps the sun, if luck
should shine from your heart
mi corazón, the luck I miss
between strands of your golden hair?

Will you give me the gift of luck
tonight, my love, *la botella*
pouring Chilean Malbec
into your hand-heated glass

la estrella bearing your name
close by the belt of Orion
as you sit upon my denim couch
in my cottage in Santa Cruz?

Will you give me the gift of love
tonight, my luck, sure in your smile?
Or will you hand me *la pera*
on a note riddled with despair

because you have waited too long
in the hand of a criminal
la mano, who bleeds your passion
leaving your face pale and wounded?

Will I give you *la luna*
the gift of lovers, blood orange
rising over the eastern bay
on this sandy cloud burned night

lightly covering your eyes
with *la corona*, the hat of kings

as you drift quiet into dreams
or will I simply watch you sleep

at a distance, through eye of mind
as I walk the beach reading poems
of love to your sleeping heart?
You, *la rosa*, I want you, come.

Then we will make our lottery
you and me, luck of our casting
cards of our making, unfolding
our joyous riddles with delight.

ephemere

tangible evidence
of a muted cornet
playing in rain

around the corner
above the bodega
through stained

sheer curtains
billowing past
broken glass

fronting a cold
water flat
between C

and D
from the bathtub
in the kitchen

beneath the rusted
tin ceiling
doesn't last

Broken Sandwiches

Broken sandwiches on a dog-eared night.
Her convolute eyes track me illucid.
Edges shine in this cataracted
Vision, emptying each kestrel's core.

As if no creature could have straight motive.
I wonder what brought her to occlusion
A less than measured means of thwarting
Contact that authors responsible choice.

She kills truth as indelicate razor
Not in clean, second-smile making cuts
In small swipes, rather, her blade un-stropped
Fashioning a tangle of clots and splits

An un-fractal spatter on canvas
So different from the life through pain drips
I used to watch on wide rectangles
Seeing order under the lies at home.

The Underwater Typewriter

She found me gathering urchins in the cove
at the feet of towering yellow kelp
rising quick to the surface with a stone
to crack the captured quarry on my chest
as I rode the pulsing swell off Point Lobos.

"Your whiskers are grey. You must have stories,"
she laughed, trailing me like a hungry gull.
"Tell me your tales, and the ways of Big Sur
while the sun still sparkles on these waters."
I opened with legends of the Ohlone

told her of great grizzlies fishing the streams
of stocky, square-rigged galleons carrying
explorers and settlers up the coast
of families who tended the Point Sur Light
of writers, of hermits of medicine men

of musicians and poets and ranchers
and thieves, high in the Santa Lucias.
"You seem to know a lot about humans,"
she whistled, splashing with her hind flippers.
"Perhaps you will write it all down for me."

I turned, diving deep into the kelp bed.
When I reached the ocean floor, she was there
laughing gently, opening her seal coat
placing a round-keyed Royal typewriter
in a rock cradle, incanting, "please begin."

perchance

My dreams populate night
with exhausting violence
wrenching pins in my limbs
jerking me hard awake
the pain so loud I scream
then, ashamed, cast about
for a quiet pillow
discovering nothing
but grey and building creaks
I keen for daylight drift

I yearn for reverie
the lazy space to shift
in diffuse curtain light
happily more awake
in opening daydream
than in the slog-a-day
life I now inhabit
so pressed for resources
i can no longer sing
a hopeful melody

I feel myself smaller
the spaces between bone
diminishing each night
my sleep window shrinking
my tumored knee aching
to lay down unhindered
to swing like a free hinge
as I lope over hills
my body disappearing
my mind becoming air

I cannot raise the strength
to summon the day dream
that allowed me to know
the world without border

bound everywhere I look
by sadistic moments
that take my living self
with complete disregard
and toss it into walls
no matter what I do

I'm too old to bargain
there are no deals with god
those younger deals I made
bought me another day
of imagining love
that could replace neglect
so I could bear up
without having to leave
something to be conjured
but magic never worked

so now I won't bear up
I know the love's not there
I won't bargain to stay
I won't bargain for love
I will just imagine
that perhaps I can dream
in daylight once again
and draw to me the light
blacked by cruelty and loss
that, when young, I let go.

Night

I kiss the night
because I have
no one else.

She responds
languid, smooth.

I relish the liquid
tumble
into her
timeless
opening.

She scares me
when I brace
and stand
apart, aware
but unwilling
to look in
refusing
to enter
continuing
to tumble
till she tears
with a streak
and dissolves
into grey light.

She warms
me, holds
me round
when I embrace
and enter her
relinquishing
reserve
tumbling
deep into

her folds
relishing
the milky
drop.

By now,
you would
think I
would just
give and go
no urge
no impulse
to teeter on
the edge
fighting
her embrace.

By now
you would
think I
would amble
easily into
that liquid
trust
knowing her
as I do
simple
and simply.

And yet
nothing
and I mean
nothing
is harder.

Seeing

For a moment, on the ledge, beyond the pine
I looked down on Sheffield Plain and toed Bear
Rock—grey, flecked, prismatic wheels spinning
off its jigs and jags, warm on my soles, and solid
I liked the hard edge of forest, preserved for now
as hedgerow to hikers' trail, falling hard from Eagle's
Perch, on Raceback Ridge, to this gentle plateau
and detested the cut pines I found one year to mark
for fools the point of vista, as if opening to light required
a context crudely framed by the forester's axe.

In those days Berkshire valleys saw no haze—inversion
layers were for Angelenos, and, closer by, people stuck
between New Haven's East and West Rocks, Sleeping
Giant snoring purple out back. I saw now the yellowing
air of that congested harbor town, and lost firm contact
with the transparent beauty of this, my place, then returned
awakened by a gnat, and in my thin-boned frame understood
that I would come back here always, in light and in dreams
and finally in death, my ashes to be scattered over this settled
plain, from high on this ledge, the one safe spot of my youth.

Shake

I walked a line a thousand milligrams of morphine long
my bowels withdrawing into my head, as if all pain
could be retained in the bunged cavities, between my cock
and my top. All I had to do to make this plan work

was let the urine swell my blocked bladder and run
backward, blowing the hell out of my distended kidneys
leaving me bloated, belly white and completely silent
but truth be told, I didn't want to shut the fuck up. Now

I had things to say, so I took a catheter and peed
like a motherfucking waterfall over the railed gurney
into a great plastic bag, flat like a stingray, whose tail
burned the shit out of my aforementioned, now inverted

cock, caked with blood, and Betadine, and stringy plastic goop
of unknown origin, flaking and peeling like a fako
skin—you know the kind you squeeze from a bottle that melts tears
in your outer layers, unbridgeable by butterflies

into a passable seal that keeps your inner layers safe
from public exposure, because god knows what the public
would think if they saw what was inside; better to saw
you at the root, give a little push, and hope that you fall

then ever come to see what's really inside, and if you stand
up to these trips, these cuts, these hacks, these patchings, these druggings
these muggings, if you stand up on your walker and shout "FUCK"
at the top of your lungs, your bowels will open, and your

piss will drain, and your nose will run and your eyes will water
and you will not retain the pain of those who would see you dead
rather than allow you to give up their closeted ghosts.
You will cry! You will scream! You will shake till there is no more.

Becoming

They're doing well these apples of the sun
riding in cars, resting in crispers, walk-in
freezers, and on counters, firm skinned, awaiting
honey, and the cold slice that comes before.

They don't fear the blade, these sun hard apples.
They know a parting will end their journey
in the round, juiced, skinned, stemmed fibrous form
given them by tree, water, dirt and light.

They know the time of becoming smaller
cannot be forestalled, and they do not care.
They will be in pieces, sweetened and bit
and mashed and digested, a memory

barely, in conscious mind, but deep in cell
these fine apples that will soon cease to be.
And their skins are bright, colors dancing
inviting the bite that will bring union

so complete it does not raise a whisper.

To Shore

Three times around the world we travelled
on our little raft made of bolsters
clothed in saggy grey on grey fabric

taken from my grandmother's Brooklyn
resting now at 815 Whitney
on the hook rug we made our ocean

The stories we'd tell in our pin cords
imagining they were sailor's pants
as we rounded Capes Horn and Good Hope

all between end of school and dinner
of shark attacks and albatrosses
we knew well enough never to shoot

as they led us in succession North
on steady winds from our mislaid course
through towering bergs and icy chop

rogue waves sixty feet or more, cresting
while we rode untouched in the furrows
into warmer waters, and made land

an atoll with three trees and pirates
from whom we stole yodels and ring dings
returning stealthily to our raft ·

to devour moonlight provisions
lashings quick loosening on our raft
waves pushing the bolsters wide apart

threatening to end us before our time
we luckless, frightened young mariners
shouting to each other over wind

"Grab that rope!" "Pull it tight!" "I'm slipping!"
"Reach! Reach! Harder!" "Don't let go!" "Save me!"
Holding tight now cross the flimsy raft

We drifted cold and silent, binding
to each other with skinny arms
until quieter, we sailed to shore.

Gittel

A large mass grew in her chest
It filled her bosom
Pushed against her ribs

When they cut away
Her breast and muscle
Her shoulder sagged

Her head dropped too
And pulled to the side
Then her chin cocked

And her eyes lifted
With the knowledge
That things could change

dropping

The moon and I
tell each other lies
this marked card night.

"We've come to this?"
he says, spitting
reflected light

in a bucket
on the heaving
wood-warped dock.

We tell, each
other lies
the moon and I

sometimes in warm
jest, toweled men
in a Russian

steam room, filling
white plastic pails
with cut hoses

sometimes in stakes
races, rising
in amplitude

and fake venom
till one, or the other
becomes laughter

shaking the vacuum
through which sound
cannot travel.

When the moon knows
you can shit him
to convulsions

he wishes he had
arms to wrap round
your wounded shoulders.

When the moon knows
you bring light
to the lying night

that you make love
he drapes a tallis
over your sorrow

beams dropping
knotted tsitsis
fraying at dawn.

Broken Lines

I look to pass, always.

A car in front

insults my throttle.

A broken yellow line

invites use.

Dash, dash, dash—

"Go fast now!

Pass that fucker!

Here's your invitation to drive

on the left side."

Use it.

It's a limited time offer,

A limited space offer

going fast (as you).

Think!

Slight pressure—your foot bearing down—

can compress time in space

bring you closer

to light.

You will be younger

        truly

            if you forget overdrive,

                if you accelerate, now, hard."

"Does that fraction

        of a moment

            matter?"

                I wonder

as I smoke

        American steel.

Double barrel yellows

        don't speak to me.

I run their silent curves in waning light

            nothing left to pass

                but time.

A Part

Her owner-less sleeve, silk filaments
loosed by the hundreds at torn shoulder
weakened and waving, balling, fraying
loses its sense of her calm white skin

the small hairs on her forearm that bent
on contact with its cream colored weave.
Her owner-less sleeve, unnerved, in air
collapses and billows, folds and twists

in contact now with itself, unfilled
an accidental windsock, severed
from its purpose, its corpus, its life
inanimate as a thing of use.

Her owner-less sleeve, a translucent
wraith, sailing on gusts, enjoys her glow
knowing surely she will go to earth
where light will fall but will not fill her

where she will be less than a remnant
dirtied and mildewed and tattered, rent
once, and soon to be forgotten.
Her owner-less sleeve, unwinding.

doubling

you enter my life in small moments
as seeds infiltrate the ground, encased
waiting to be opened by water

strangely, they find home in me
rooting, spreading, unfolding inside
until I feel them poke at my eyes

express themselves lively through my skin
tickle my nostrils, and part my lips
now abuzz with words meant only for you.

Anacoluthon

failure follows,
following failure
of self.

fallow
now.

following dis-informs
out-forms, dysforms,
if en-trailed in other.

string
pulled.

consequent, following
temporal antecedent
says nothing.

moment
empty.

failure to follow,
what now?

prescribed
sequence?

logic?

authority?
(whose)?

grammatic convention?
(a gathering)?

failure leads,
following failure
of self.

fertile
now?

The Poet's Chair

Meri, you don't know the poet's chair
where I've spent many a year
when others weren't here
above City Lights
atop the stair
hoping you
were near

Notch Road in February

Coming up Notch Road in February
Past 1950s suburban houses
Past the hill shredded with construction
Past the steep, coarse, pine needle watershed
In late afternoon, snowshoes and parka

It's seventeen below with the wind chill
And as the sales agent from Williamstown
And I shuffle into Boney's old lands
The sky is effaced by towering bark
And the snow, ice crusted on the surface

Breathes in the cold and shows itself dark
I'm falling into a bank now, four feet deep
Dropping backward into powder, adrift
In a puff of snow, for less than a breath
Before I arrive at something solid

Head below my feet, knowing I can't stand
As the snow closes in, frosting my face
I feel slow; time has developed texture
It rubs my cheeks and works into the down
Is this time or cold? There's no difference now.

Coffee

The sun comes, nearly all
A surprise this November
Morning in an unfamiliar bed

Crossing my lids
Opening and rolling
Me onto my back.

Unbroken light
No darker than robin's egg
Fills the half moon picture plane

Beneath which, I was told
Volunteer firemen
Once drove their trucks

I see now I have been sleeping
In a parking place, soon to be
Removed, a temporary occupant

Behind now, and below
I hear soft feet, the spill
Of water, and the sharp

Clank of pot on stove
Soft feet again
And I'm back asleep

The air warms, I smell
Coffee. My lips broaden
The skin falls from my face

Spreading into the pillow
Not giving a stirring
Twitch to daybreak.

Feet arrive, deliberate
Carrying coffee
Filling my nose with prospect

II

The thin, fold-out mattress
Depresses to my left

She sits facing me
Legs crossed under

Cup and saucer
Elevated

Her brown hair finer
And lighter

Than I had
Remembered

III

Steam from the coffee
Rises below her gouache
Skin—clear, unlined
Gentle and elegant
Beneath tipple grey eyes

I see her face truly
For the first time
Complexion and clarity
Of morning lake water
Cool, rounding, un-rippled

She tells me about the cup
It's old glazed markings

Then follows my eyes
Up to the second reflection
Of light playing on water

IV

I watch its darting display
All white and shadow
And neglect to see

The broken surface
Of her face. "I have to
Get something," she says.

V

I rise, hoist trou, pull a thick
Faded moss shirt over
My head, feeling its
Threads snag and release
As they cross my unshaved
Face. I stand, barefoot

In the bathroom, hoping
To clean up, but she
Is in the short hall, tears
Dropping slowly, pooling
On her lower lids, as we
Move into the kitchen

VI

I rub her thick
Unmuscled arm
Through thin fabric
All grief, she takes

My hand, letting go
For a moment
Of her, as yet
Unmourned mother

VII

I hold her hand—her fingers,
Long, skilled, bent in gentle arc
Pressing against my rougher skin

I cup her cheek, feeling the cold
Spill of death, barely washing
From her ducts. She turns

Thick and solid, into me
And we rock, in the chill
November morning air

VII

"What do you want?"
Says she, now composed

"Just coffee. Black,"
Says me, who never drinks

I need the bitterness
The metal, filtered, clank

Of grounds on yellowed teeth
To take me.

By Which

The scars peppering your back are shrinking.
The opaque wash coating your pale irises
grey, in moments you remain unseen
recedes faster and more frequently now.

You've become familiar with letting go
your mask, the dropping of your guard taking
the line of ritual newly learned.
Without the pattern it would not happen.

We both know that. Yet, whether you follow
the thread is never a given. We must
discover, in each taut moment, the means
to continue, and it isn't easy.

I so want to break with this ritual
to pull you close and smash all that binds you
to peel the scars from your back, the fibers
surrounding your heart, the enigmatic

shell into which your face withdraws, and kiss
your fresh pink skin, your eyes hiding nothing
your heart unhusked, unbound, completely mine
no interval between your appearance

and arrival. and because I love you
I forgo the violent urge to have you
other than you are, and open, instead
to you and to the ritual by which we meet.

A Common Occurrence

On Thursday Kara wept, rolled to the gutter, inhaled exhaust,
felt February in aching stria, faced grimed granite, intimate
interstice cleaving her from stone, and wondered what wear
her water would wind into the precision cut rock. "Curbstones
were better," she thought, "when hewn, not sliced.   Remember

Troy before concrete sidewalks, giant paving stones
lining the streets of that broken place, where I would lie
on my back, dripping ice-cream from a fractured wafer
cone onto the blue-stone, soaking in heat; watching
my small, sugared dairy river advance by stutters
till it tumbled from the edge, my Niagara in miniature,
to pitted asphalt four inches below.   I always wonder,

'Who am I asking to remember?' I'm alone now and
cold. Yet, as I lie here in the street in front of the taxi
stand, I hear myself say, 'Remember,' as if I can walk
with someone who knows me, back to a common place,
as if someone will be there to receive what I have to share,
as if my someone would lift me up, pour me steaming tea
and listen intently. I hear myself say, 'remember,'

to open ears that are not there, because I cannot bear
the echo of unclaimed meaning.   I cannot bear
witness to myself, if all I felt stops here.

I hear myself say, 'remember,' and wish the sound
to cross my lips, which chapped and pressed stay
still. I wonder, 'who was I just talking to?'

No matter. 'Remember how our room boiled at night?'"
Kara curled against the low stone, hugging it as pillow,
asked forgiveness, smiled to the frost burning her cheek—
"no more distance to travel," she thought, and went to sleep.

requiem for a spoken word

it hung for a moment in air and echo
decayed into ambient hush, as the
next word was spoken, a noise overlaid
on the dwindling moment of meaning

this one word, from this one voice, held in this
one room, in front of this one audience
made of many faces and twice the ears
open, receptive, tympanic membranes

vibrating, sympatico with the song
so rapidly expired, a firefly
in sound, and yet its timbral light lingered
in the note, in the color, in the heart

of one who unexpectedly opened
on its voicing, and, now, vulnerable
in this room of strangers, unconsciously
mourned its passing from air to memory.

Inflection

I feel the ebbing tide
I know its pull
I know if I let
it go

I will soon discover
sparkling sand
seaweed
shells

Sea-glass, stones and wonders
I know I will miss them
when it returns

Still, I fear
the ebbing.

Out

I suppose I am out now,
out of excuses, out of art,
out of contrivance, out.

Out of lies to myself,
out of places to hide,
just out, exposed,
naked and ugly,
and it's a fucking relief.

I always thought gay
people had it easy—
of course they do not—
because they couldn't
duck the issue, as easily
as people like me who have
other aspects of themselves
that will make them hated
simply for being, that are easier
and more deadly to hide.

So I am out, naked and ugly,
and I make some people's skin
crawl when I tell them my truths,
and I don't disclose all of myself
to many people who call themselves
my "friend," because they don't want really
to hear me, to listen, to know me in my all,
and yet they are good enough friends
to keep around, and I am, in some strange
way, better for knowing them, better for having
partial relationships, kaleidoscopic communion.

Then there are the people who want to know me,
naked and ugly, who don't flinch, who offer comfort
and wisdom and support, and who rally round my cause,
'cause they are fellow travelers, open and compassionate
and real, completely real. They would not exist were I not out.

It's funny that, in and out—fucking. When you are in, you have a pass,
and you hold onto that pass as tightly as a kid clutching a magic ticket,
but all of you is in and the more you are in, the more you contract. Inclusion
is enclosure and you are fenced, bound by assent and destined to atrophy even
as you relish your insider status, your belonging, your possession by others, as you
dispossess yourself. When you are out, there ain't no pass, ain't no free ride, ain't no
admission to the magic circle, and you can spend so much time banging your head against
the wall, trying to get in. And if you are clever enough to gain admission, you find when you arrive
that the circle is empty. Exclusion is exposure and once exposed you, negative, cannot make positive
what is hollow, no matter how hard you try. So if you stay in, which you never were or could be, having been
out, you will dessicate—lovely. I outsider have been in, and it nearly killed me, not metaphorically. I repeat it nearly
killed me. So I came out, and now every day I'm raw, naked, ugly and exposed, vulnerable and vital and breathing
and seeing and scared to death. Ironic that, don't you think, scared to death but living, invulnerable and dying. There's
that in word again. Only the dead are truly invulnerable and what's the fun of that? So now I am out raising hackles and fears,
and dropping love like gumdrops, and feeling so fucking vulnerable because love scares people and giving it without condition
is the scariest fucking thing of all, and I am out and not at all clear, and out and about and seeing things I rather would not.

And there is strange justice in that, seeing it all, feeling it all and not letting it condition me in any way, learning to hold on as best
I can to nothing, and that, refusing to cling, staying out, trapezing off the side of a small boat on hard tack in high wind, is the hardest
thing of all, and it's fucking wonderful, and now that I am out I hope that I never forget it, and that by example I teach it to my boy
as I was never taught, and that he savors being out, struggles never to enter the hollow ring, and lives rich and full every day of his life.

MARC ZEGANS

horseshoes

when the light started to linger
we'd walk out to the horseshoe pits
my dad in his cotton plaid shirt
coast guard regulation cut hair

me veering toward the clouds of dust
and the clang of shoe on rebar
watching the old men knock leaners
into the dirt, matching ringers

drinking miller, bud, pabst and schlitz
smoking lucky strikes and viceroys
doctor approved cigarette brands
in the year of jfk's death

the year after my grandfather's
I was told I'd made him happy
but that my mother's pregnancy
with my soon to be born brother

was really what mattered to him.
it signaled, according to her
the future of the family
which in her eyes I never was.

I was there to serve my brother
to take care of him while she slept
but when my dad came home from work
we'd amble out and watch men pitch.

Inversion

Stunted silver birch
Leafless, as if inverted
Life below cool soil

These days

These days I'm taking the subway at night.
Where to? That's a good question. I'm not sure.
It bumps and clangs beneath the East River
Where in 1912 my grandfather swam

Amidst the flotsam, sewerage and rats
Running the lines to ships which still dotted
The Southern point of that thin seaport town
A finger in the stream gathering life

From confining quarters left fast at night
by grimy people possessed of nothing
but the will to move to water parting
Mica schist, piled high at Northern end

A cradle for rathskellers and blind pigs
And more bodies than the night can count
A thousand kids on my block he would say
A thousand kids, 50 for each six months.

But childhood ended long before then.
I was running papers at age fourteen
From Canal to Fourteenth Street for Fairchild
They're across the street from where we now live

Can you imagine that? Fairchild's still here
And I'm across the street in a high rise
with a balcony, hot and cold water
And two bathrooms in which to enjoy it.

The buildings of my youth are all gone now
I like walking there amidst the rubble though
Taking you East on an old fashioned stroll
Through the job shops in what they call Soho

Now that lofts are filled with paint splattering
renters and manufacture has moved South
Right-to-work states meaning freedom to starve.
We got rid of that and the jobs went too

These days

Look at the metalwork on these buildings
I remember when none of this was rust
When black gloss drenched the proud iron columns
That fronted for a system of piecework

On which fortunes were made on broken backs.
I'm not sure this will make sense to you
What is gained and what is lost over time
In this place where memory lives in cracks

And the building that housed mother's restaurant
is rubble. I can show you the bricks though
and tell you stories of my father's wine
which he made in vats far below the street

And sold by the gallon to fat Burghers
Who ate large steaks, ends flopping off the plates
And shouted loudly for second helpings
And died young from eating this healthy food.

I'm not sure this will make sense to you
But I imagine you will remember
And somehow put your memory to use
And think of me swimming in the East River

Hoping that my shirt would be on the dock
After I climbed the pilings to return
To my block of thousands and my long walks
Carrying bundles on the Lower East Side.

These days I'm taking the subway at night
Letting the train carry me to Brooklyn
and early memories of Ocean Avenue
Set by a boy who swam the East River

And somehow I have let these things make sense
In the course of forty years, as I watch
memory opening in the deep cracks
inscribed on this ride to where I'm not sure.

Three Milagros

For my heart
For my insight
For my manhood

For the moments when I am asked to relinquish these things
For the moments when avarice and fear threaten to overwhelm
For the moments when I must walk alone

For my heart
For my insight
For my manhood

For the moments when I must make myself sturdy
For the moments when I must eschew certain reward
For the moments when I must accept danger

For my heart
For my insight
For my manhood

For the moment when three pieces of greening brass
And the faith of an old love must count above all else.

A Hipster Retires

Do you remember the days when it meant something

to be a hipster? When sunglasses

worn over Benzedrine eyes in nightclubs

in the subterranean precincts

Of the West Village, where thirty dollars

paid your rent, was not an ironic

quasi-historical, counter cultural

reference to post-vernacular

psedo-American sartorial

style, but a way to keep your fucking bloodshot

eyes safe from the scintilla of light

reflecting off the bell of Cannonball's

horn, so you could follow his solos

deep into the heart of a place no one

had ever been, and never again would see?

Do you remember when manifestos

written on Royals, white-out corrected

shared by hand, and read only by a few

could, by their dangerous sentiments

change in a moment the national discourse

rallying the voices of free love and free speech

and the possibility of moments

explored, consciousness expanded—the bomb

hanging above yellow and black fallout

markers—when to be hip meant to be brave

to be hip to the truth that power denies

to be knowing of the shadow pulsing

in the night of our American soul

to give birth to the cool and forget it

as soon as Miles turned his back on stage

because a change was gonna come

real soon; when to be hip was to be invested

with one's brothers in defiant meaning

knowing always, that our blood could be spilt

by nightsticks and fists and fruitless war?

Do you remember those times as you wear

your too tight plaid shirts, drink your PBRs

sport your skinny jeans, ape trailer culture

in Disneyfied neo-bohemia

while you entwine yourself, unwitting

in neo-fascist social networks

a happy creative economy insider?

If you do, I applaud your ironic

self-awareness. As for me, I've no need

to be hip to the inside joke

my time is short, there's hearts to be won

the time has come for our hipster to retire.

# of a door

you bit your lower lip, letting your hand fall
from the belt of your robe, arm extending
carrying with it proscenium fronting
curtain, as you stood in the stained wood frame

of a door built generations before
one of many facing maids' corridor
showing shadows as you released your lip
drawing me cross the threshold onto your bed

your buckthorn berry spying dress slipping
from the foot, sounding the roughness of silk
piling, a lost sheath; the cover story
forgotten amidst the flesh, I suspect.

would that night be less valuable to me
less direct, if we had met under cover?

Trip

I died three deaths last night, laid out against the sheets, breathless cooling corpse
my forehead clammy to her warm hand. I died three deaths last night, letting life
gases rise from my skin not wizened, smooth, stilling. I died three deaths last night
in waking horror and watched the circled hell of what had been unbind and begin
a diaspora, spreading above my blank and shuttered eyes, uncoupled memories,
if that, drifting apart—the story of me as broken man now dissolved, unconstructed.

At each death last night I heard a child's rattle, silver and distant, and the dry shakes
of ancient men, breathing alone on hospital beds in cotton johnnies, and the rough
rasp foretelling venomous strike, or so it could have been. At each death, I heard
the rustle of my sheets and the hiss of air through blunted teeth, uncusped remains
of five thousand troubled nights. At each death, I heard the now unstifled screams
the cries that no longer could reside in the skin, the muscle, the fascia, the bone.

At each passing moment, now alone, I became less grave, less determined, less
severe—there was nothing to hold back. At each passing moment I smiled more
kindly, each death a simple grace. At each passing moment I wondered why
I had not come to this place sooner, and at the last I came to love my foolish self.

Bastard's Song

Illegitimate I, in wedlock born,
enter life an accident—
so claim my makers.

As if their unconsidered act,
their neglect of consequence,
their fear of liability, for a life

thoughtlessly conceived
confers authority to assign
cause.

Illegitimate I, in wedlock born,
in a deterministic universe
cannot be accident.

Illegitimate I, in wedlock born,
If, by intent, life fills untended cracks,
cannot be an accident.

Illegitimate I, in wedlock born,
in a world of chosen meaning,
can be accident, only if I say so.

And yet for them it is convenient
to call my inconvenient self
an accident.

I hope, in this new life,
I do not believe them.

San Diego

We stare at the surf
at the end of longer days
beyond the breakers

She lies on the sand
I return to the sharp waves
that swept up my son

We stand on the cliff
The sound of surf dragging rocks
is her gift to me

Toby's 19th hole
late in the morning for eggs
We enjoy the grease

In Balboa Park
A fantasy of old Spain
We walk hand in hand

Pollo Asada
under the tarp at Tower 3
I head for the waves

She at Tower 3
Me in late winter waves
sucked under, alone

Her house is repaired
Landscaping is made complete
so she can leave

Cheap Chinese massage
in a strip mall far away
Li Li rubs her feet

Good chips at Lucha
The only place I drink Orange Bang
She brings tequila

Letters to Nora
Read under the influence
in Wills' fine shop

I'm dying inside
Nothing will stop the bleeding
except for your kiss

leaving

the land under my eye is swollen like an elephant
I'm grey and sag, loss lines covering my body, my time
past a wrinkle, and underneath I see the thin muscled
turn of a supple body yearning to shed the hiding history
to move again with grace and power across old bones

this is happening now, the walk to second life, across
the scarring fields, from under the interment, out beyond
the gravity of the sucking east, a hole from which lighter
than I was, but heavier than when I came, I now depart.

Sheets

You weren't disposed to notice
a made bed, sheets unwrinkled
by a child missing from his room
on nights when you were out.

You weren't disposed to notice
his footed pajamas tangled
in your soiled bedclothes
on mornings of your return.

You weren't disposed to notice
bruises and cuts and bleeding
and stifled tears and silence
held so long it pained his mouth

to speak. As sailors you failed
to notice telltales, small strings
blowing true, and so you never
could handle a boat under sail.

You weren't disposed to notice
that he watched the small signs
and tacked happily into the wind
on Long Island Sound: alone.

Chutes Chaudières: Ashuapmushuan

Portage

          At cliff's edge

The soil gives

          Then you

Cry trailing

          Skin scraped hands

And knee bangs

          Through sun-bleached

Blue jeans

          Stained with aluminum

You look up

          Water falls

The air
          Is clear

Blood and dirt

          Mix thick

On your fingers

          Cliff-face and stream

Up or die

    It's simple

So you rise

    Hauling pack

Grabbing rock

    Pulling deep

From your gut

    As your tin cup

Tearing loose

    Falls into the chute.

Passing

Moving through death
Unwinding cell and stem
Introduces slowness and spread.

Moving through death—giving up
heat, gently uncoupling, allowing
space to come between structures
once purposive, now in decay.

Moving through death
Un-mixing hope and sorrow
Discovering the kind turn
When all is received.

Walking Out

Your wrinkle skin
on bones thin
bagged your veins
like wire in a trunk

You shuddered
and hacked

Black spittle
rolled down
your lip

And you
let it drop
onto your
flimsy
blue and white
print gown

You hacked again
your dark eyes
large like a baby's

looked past us
staring at ghosts
which limned

your memory
now bigger
than any vision

you could field

Hungry still
voracious
and unsated

you stared into the void
from which you had walked
and compared it to the one

you would enter

"One step," you thought
"One step when I have taken

 so many

How can I fear walking into
a secure embrace
an embrace so much

stronger than that from which
I was torn as a child?
a powerful embrace

that cannot be broken
by black-booted officers
come to take a serving boy

How can I be scared of that
which I always wanted?"

Voracious and unsated
you let your head fall to your chest
dark eyes unfocused and filled with water

The ghosts filed past you
watching slowly
one for each footprint

you left on the Steppe

"Why are they always silent?" you wondered
"I can see them, but they won't speak
There are so many, so many sliding past
so many. Can't one stop to speak?"

I heard your question
and knew you needed proper reason

proper reason to give account

So I stepped forward
I who had never met you before
I who had only heard the stories
and moved with shy deliberation
into your field of vision

"Small and dark,
unlike the rest

Who was this new ghost?"
you puzzled

It turned to face you
unsteady but square
and began to speak

It asked you about your journey
You listened to its question
and a smile edged
onto the corner
of your mouth
as the images
became rich
with color

"I used to make maps," you said
"maps in my head

Then one day

When I had made
all the maps
I could make

I picked myself up
and started to walk."

Incantation

We tire so easily,
you and I,
us strong people.

We look the world
in the eye,
you and I,
us strong people.

It nearly kills us,
you and I,
us strong people.

We don't die,
you and I,
us strong people.

We are wracked
with pain,
you and I,
us strong people,

and moved to anguish,
you and I,
us strong people,

by the brutality
of life,
you and I,
us strong people.

And we survive,
over and over,
you and I,
us strong people.

We are broken

on the wheel,
you and I,
us strong people.

And we survive,
you and I,
us strong people,

and we manage
to love,
you and I,
us strong people.

Unclasped

At Steep Ravine I took you into surf
your fear breaking faster than the hard waves
spit and sparkle, lips, teeth, lids and brown hair
bouncing as you jumped in the shore breaks

Waves rising, dancing round your thighs, foaming.
I took your hand in the hollow between
two curls and led you to deeper waters.
You looked back to shore, scanning for your boy

A thin line of love tethering you to shore
You would not go beyond the second break.
The line, a kite string too long, would be cut
if you ducked with me into the black swell.

Your arm extended, holding me, fingers
unclasping slowly, at last releasing
as I turned my young back to your kind face
diving into the cold quiet beneath.

Running

On Thursday she wept in my car
parked in the busy lot outside
the twenty-four hour drugstore.

I bought her tissues and sat
quiet in my leather seat.
Her mascara did not run.

II

That evening, late, after she
had been feted between
anniversary of a dead marriage

and birthday signifying
the end of fertility
taken for granted

we made love.
It seemed necessary
dangerous and complete.

III

On Friday, we slept late
and overhung with longing
and tired tissues, made love
again, quiet and still.

We spent the day together
and apart and celebrated
her birthday, on my floor
eating Chinese and drinking
old wine, fragile nose, delicate
on the lips, and I remembered
the year, because I had gone
to Rio then, and swept to sea

overlooking Vidigal, by D
I could have stayed
but faithful in my vows
I remained thirteen
years in hell.

Again we made love,
long time, and I wept.

IV

On Saturday, in bed
till four, and then out
she to celebrate her
birthday gone with
her red-headed
friend and rival
and me to mix
tapes, blues
for a broken
heart.

This night we
did not make
love, but held
close against
each other
and woke
solid in each
other's arms.

Hacking

Soft in hand, polished threads
smooth with age, my green
hunting jacket, no longer warm,
inner wool, flat, thinned, matted
hangs bare, like me.

Air rises between me
and the coat, stained
orange. What does
it say about me
that I wear this pen
splotched relic
out and about?

I wonder
if the woman
on my arm
will notice
the stain.

trimming

sometimes the break of ice burdened limbs
cracks like gunshot across these stark woods
the fall of branch and twig silent, until
snow muffled impact sounds an end to growth

the limbs, summer and fall, have been dropping
silent to the ground, an unseen ice storm
weighing them beyond what can be bourn
a blockage of flow unnatural in warmer

months, or perhaps a reminder that loss
imported fruit, de-stems regardless
of season, displacing expectation
the better to achieve its cutting shock

the limbs, summer and fall, have been dropping
there is nothing I can do except watch
them fall away and wonder at the speed
of the trimming that leaves nothing but core.

almost

you haven't seen my danger body
it's different than you remember
it takes smaller steps, shoulders turned
head forward, chest concave

You cannot see my danger body
gristle sagging beneath my eyes
meat-hooked from my cheekbones
once stretchers for my supple skin

now begging for a creak and groan
to mark the aching weight, carried
cross the unwind of suns and moons
you do not see the self-eating monster

gorging on my tired, tattered brain
diving eel-like into my guts
nor do I, but I feel his teeth
bite by bite, and the turn to mush

it hurts to see yourself digested
by a parasite you cannot expel
that is the part my danger body
learned to let go, so it could live

observant, aware, guarded and shocked
my danger body separate from me
a tiny voice lost in this chasm
of bone and skin and failing parts

you do not know my danger body
but you do know me, now, almost.

as she

I'm feeling old pain tonight
she's walking with me
slow, steady, regular

I feel her in my eyes
I always feel her there
rimming the sockets

deep and muscular
in a small way

I feel her in the bones
beneath my cheeks
drawing down my eyes

that have seen too much
in a small day

I feel her now, talking to me
she has a clear voice
this pain, not one to glory

this pain, and I don't
want to let her go

I don't want my eyes
to wash out, my cheeks
to rise and my lips to turn

to smile. Something
familiar will be gone

And so little is familiar
to me now, on my stroll
with this haunting

fine haired girl

so little is familiar

I let go her hand
before the door
and feel her walk away

silent and bewildered
having stayed with me

so many years, and air
blows between us
chills and shivers

coming slant across
my spine. My eyes

releasing now
as cheeks soften
looking forward

"Gently now. Gently now."
as she passes into night.

Starting

I ride the sea on purple curl
As night draws near

Arms back, head thrust
Leading with my jaw

Water drops and rises
As we progress, wave and I

To where it scatters on sand
In turbulent wash

II

I roll in the froth
Stand like a dog; shake
Water from my head

Turn my back
On the darkening
Beach and scrubby hills

Look out to the sun
Puddled sea, which slips
Inviting, between my toes

I run out again, plunge and swim
Duck diving under the swells
Each time I surface

The light has drifted.
A locomotive pumping, I stroke
Huge whistle bursting my lips

III

Out; out into the white light
Dancing on the ocean, last reach

Of setting sun. Out; out

Into the magic pool
As if I could follow
All the way to China

And then I reach its edge
Marveling at how fine
A line it paints

On wrinkled chop
As I survey its arc
Cold water at my back

I feel a tide pull my chest
Ripping my toes

IV

I give over
Letting it carry me
Out toward the light

Out toward the last orange
Splash on open sea
And there we play, light and I

Dancing and laughing, on water-top
As I turn corkscrews in the waves
We kiss goodnight, as she slides

Under water covers
Then I turn, surveying
The distant black contour

I put my head down
Taste the salt
And start to swim.

Catch

I guess I went in summer to the concrete pier
To cast my line with the homeless anglers
To watch it arc, then drop, into the troubled bay

I guess I went to lean against the rusting rail
To troll for stripers coursing black below the swells
I guess I went to feel the fog wet my face

To watch for yellow bridge lights above lonesome horns
I guess I went in summer to breathe deep cold air
To sit, watching my rod. I guess I went for hope

And when it bent, the moonlight anglers' faces rose
The fish in plastic buckets thrashed, and I hauled back
Watching its hooped end bounce and dive before I reeled

I ran the line, reeled again, playing tug until
I drew him out, black-eyed, blunt-nosed, his grey skin rough
In my hands, as I cut and threw him to the salt.

Finding

Your lids low, as if two moons had descended
so near they covered the bare night sky
tiny star bands singing bright below your lashes.

It takes good ears to hear the sound of light
A stillness in the heart to sound your eyes
dropping line below the receding whisper
into the quiet layer, finding ground.

One Flight

Her distress left her faster than Reilly gave up the ghost.
He was lucky in that way; she not, and it gently surprised
her that an hour's rest gave her dispensation, while his
was meted out in contemplation of a nap of longer duration.

That he was in a box and she not amused her, and yet
child-eyed, at the middle, she wondered at being alive
without worry. Anxiety, that longer word for dread of future
grief, had left her naked, clean-washed, skin pink and warm,
wet hair, chilling slowly in a towel turban, and presently she
would walk out onto the street without fear. She laughed,

drying her skin and selecting clothing, now not as gird,
but as petal. She felt flush and blush, quivery and light-
footed, her heels dancing and click on the yellowed
wood floor. And day was over, and night inviting
and her lips pulled high back into her cheeks, and she
flipped her yellow hair, and remembered the days
when she and her friends rolled their skirts to draw
boys. And free again to draw at her pleasure, she
pulled shut the door, departed her aerie, and dipped
deep into the inkwell, radiant, poised and assured.

Breaking the Muse

Still one moment, absorbed and lucid, clear
of distraction, open and spilling—dreams
into air, onto paper and canvas;
drawing scents of crushed flowers, oil carried

on air by small gestures, a turn of neck
propagating waves warmly inspired,
exhaled then, carbon covering jasmine,
which lingers in caesura at breath's turn.

Elapsed time, a clock's division outside
the sustain, would mark months rolling silent
through days rising and falling frictionless,
no air impeding celestial spin.

I rise in favor of this long moment
knowing I have broken it forever.

# of you

sinkin' into dexter
he spreads his tenor
cross the night

a track of starry notes
milky light in smoke
a triplet played

a bebop line
a note hangin' time
in the corner

of memory begun
in a quiet run
in a soft room

at play with exhaustion
completely lost in
a dream of you.

Withdrawal

As a writer of plays I could not see
the lit stage, my eyes too damaged
for that. A fresnel's fixed and focused
beam emits no aura, yet I saw its penumbra
pulsing white round its black casing
and wondered if I would ever return.

My seat was empty near five years
my seat, filled with asses of others
who did not think in stage pictures
and me alone outside the theatre
wondering, would I ever return?

I could not read by incandescent light
my shades were drawn against the day
and I sat half a life, or so it felt, squinting
through sunglasses, writing in blocked
marker against gridded pulp on an easel.

Was this insane?

I felt the light outside my shade as heat
as cold in winter, as chaotic jumble
for it no longer cohered in my brain
each point, each photon distinct
and that was too much. I grew dizzy
felt myself dropping, falling from light
And so I withdrew, perhaps forever.

I did not know.

Now I sit, six rows back, on folding seat
alert, waiting. The stage fills, lights rise
beams focused, picture sharp, and I

am amazed.

Defilement

Your tragedies were too large to face
So you deferred them for a generation or more
Passing them as sacred relics on to your young.

You presented your hardships, wrapped and beribboned
On festive occasions, when family gathered
Placing them, in the guise of brilliant necklaces

Meant to bedazzle, around our throats.
The chains did not feel heavy
We did not notice their slip into wet concrete

That set hard against the vandal's chisel.
And you, who took psychotic refuge
In a future you had no right to claim

So that your world could be better ordered
Hid from your shame, as you had from your pain
And justified your transgression as sacrifice.

To the Waves

I am now blood brother to the waves
So they told me when we met at sunset
Along the wash skimmed sand at Torrey Pines
In the moment between drop and green flash

Black in the curl, white on the lip, streaked
orange in the furrows, perpendicular
to my walking watch, as I remember
the riptide and the sucking undertow

when waves were not enough to carry me
broken, spitting, dropping on my head
filling my gasping mouth and gut with brine
until I stopped calling for help and swam

as a wave of my own making, a surge
a surge atop the churn, a rise over
the relentless pull, down this shallow slope
to where the shelf ended, and deep water

blacked my eyes, ached my head, and begged me drop
into its quiet, eternal current
an easy slowing, a welcome blanket
a matching of temperature, mine and hers

I saw the desperation in her eyes
the fear that she would fail to bring me down
that I would hold my heat against her suck
releasing it into my arms and legs

each time I came up, and swam wave's cushion
penetrating water, air, light, reaching
for final shore break and beyond to land.
Showing this desperation was her gift

"Although I might get you, I don't have you
we both know that now," she said with a sigh

then pulled my legs down into weed and pulp
and water so cold, I lost all control

of muscle, chest and even my breathing
but that was for a moment, and she knew
that on the rising wave I would be hard
and fast, driving past the point of carry

and when I came to swim beyond the waves
they called me blood brother, and I left her
kneeling in the break, staggering to shore.

Old Keys

Keys that open nothing
Hang heavy on my ring

Solid and thick, grooves worn
They rub finger edge

Their touch bringing sadness
Pushing from sinuses

Welling against eyes
And the bridge of nose

A repository
For tears that never come

My focus softens
As I stroke the keys

Which opened doors
To rooms once familiar

And locked secrets
In private places

I want to be reminded
Of each key's closing moment

To remember the final sentence
In a forgotten chapter of my life

But old keys are orphans
Who cannot speak of grief.

Somerville

When I kissed her under the streetlight
in Somerville, across from the Sherman
off Union Square, I felt my feet dissolve
followed in quick succession by my knees

thighs, hips, neck, arms and head, leaving only
my lips. Lidless, I could see everything
the blue smoke surrounding her lips, drifting
cool through the space where our bodies had been

the teenagers ricocheting from light post
to light post, Bally's silver "Balls a Poppin"
before draining in a chain down Webster
the lines of cars, the strings of bars, and her

long blond hair dancing samba with the smoke.
When was the last time a girl melted me
this way, and me her, a double dissolve
into the preternaturally warm

November New England night, sea salting
her delicious, expatriated lips?
That question would have to wait for morning
because we were kissing in Somerville

B.B. King was gone, and we had the thrill.

And I Knew

the break of love
the new bleak night
the cast of dark
the end of fright

the rise above
without insight
no one to spark
or hear delight

sheer as stealth
stretched to rim
unmarked by pen
the story dim

I lost myself
abandoned him
erased, my friend
leaving only scrim

and in the end
there's never hope
a loving word
a sacred trope

the final bend
the gentle slope
you overheard
but can't emote

you leave this place
you never came
you weren't there
it's all the same

no saving face
no call for blame

And I Knew

no lion's chair
no want of shame

I saw you creep
in the light
you stole my dark
it wasn't right

I didn't steep
in your spite
beneath the stark
bedroom light

and I saw through
past your troubles
past your door
feeling you

your shaking core
your light taking
evermore
nothing solid

nothing true
and I knew
and I knew
and I knew.

Him

I remember the burn of the needle, the weight of the drip, the heat of the morphine, running up my arm from my wrist, the scratch of my skin, the rising red welts, the swelling inside my artery, drawing pain on the path where relief should have been. "He's got a morphine allergy." "Switch him?" "I guess we'd better ask him first."

I am him, here between the steel bedrails, in the flimsy blue Johnny—"Put one on back and one facing front." like it matters when they're snaking a tube up my cock, through my bladder to my kidney. It's for their relief, their modesty, not mine. It's for their comfort, their professional distance, to robe me weakly, to diminish my presence, so that they may talk about "him" without disturbing their visual field, so they may talk about "him" without considering for a moment that he has ears.

I am him, senses sharpened—pain does that you know—watching as they in Dockers and Mephistos and french blue shirts and J Crew ties and short white coats, casual professionals, confer, charts in hand, beepers on hip, photo IDs clipped or hung from their necks, signifying belonging, and distance from their patients, who are ID'd by tape on the wrist.

I am him, bruised and stented, dry-mouthed and cold.

only safety

safety glass, broken, has a crackle pattern
defining many principalities
in a space, once a clear union.

in this broken space we see green borders.
the thickness of the medium matters
more to our eyes than the barely refracted

light that once told us what was beyond it.
my car is full of broken safety glass
spattered with drops of break and enter blood

an egg-shaped grey rock stolen from a yard
sits on the floor under my steering wheel
looking confused as I was to find it.

my pricked palms and sore ass know safety glass
it doesn't feel particularly safe
the safety glass, not me; it's all broken.

I'm fine except for a few small punctures
and the feeling that I let my car down
by not having enough money to save it.

it's a classic, this pininfarina
powerful and hungry black jaguar
perfectly balanced, strong and civilized

uncared for, overdriven and neglected
before I took its wood wheel in my hands
loving it for what it was and could be

knowing that if I kept it alive
fragile and agile, burning gas and oil
that I might travel down the smoking field.

tonight, I do not know if its time has come

just as I don't know whether mine is up.
that I could not prevent this violation

nor prevent those that broke my safety glass
would once have filled me with terror and grief.
now I know, this is the way of the world

those without power lose what they cherish
in breaks, tears, cuts, spatters and pieces
long before their love would have it so.

I've lost so much that I would have held dear
in the years of care and restoration
had I been presented with such chances.

instead, I have let go of the dearest
day after day, after day, after day
learning to love more deeply in this loss.

I have no fear, only curiosity
and sorrow for the man with the rock
whose only safety lay in breaking glass.

the outgoing

I should have lived

        and I did

with nothing left

        but breath

and pain, and heart

        pounding

and the drying ache

        of salt

swamped veins

        and the

churning, wicked

        urge

to heave out the ocean

        swallowed

I should have lived

        and I did

And the college boy

                                        who went

with his girl

                                        to kiss

in the breakers

                                        did not surface

He beautiful

                                        and strong

having no skills

                                        was torn

by the rips

                                        sucked down

by the tow

                                        his great lungs

filling with sea

                                        as the

videographer

impotent

digitized his

struggle

and the girl

he came

to kiss, bobbing

in the green

space between

life and death

I had visited

three days before

and before then

as well

steaming, pounding

panic

subdued

the outgoing tide

                              exposes sand

shallowing the waters

his family

                              waits

virginia

I was four the first time I heard
the talkin' blues, round the side
of the gas station, playin' hard
through the broken radio
sittin' on the crate card table

where the good old boys spat chaw
drank "co-colas" from green bottles
thick, twisted glass, heavy in the hand
yellow boxes of empties, rusty
metal dividers segregating the bottles.

What is Hers

Grey lace, her thong hangs on the thin steel, black knob-
ended peg from my wood valet. She's left it as scent
marker, as trace memory, so I will not forget peeling
them from her cool white thighs, so I will not forget
her opening to me, so I will not forget her taste,
her tongue, her caress, her watered eyes,
her parted lips—full, reddened, younger
than her years—so I will not forget.

Hoop earrings: open-clasped, thin, bare, simple.
I thought they were silver, but laying so long
untarnished, I wonder now whether they might
be white gold—they cannot be platinum, too
warm for that—or perhaps something cheaper,
and the thought of that only deepens their elegance,
reminding me of her simplicity, her fragility, her taste.

Tiny cut glass, black beads on a crumpled brass
necklace, set deliberately under the earrings
on my French vanilla bathroom radiator.
She dropped the hoops days before
and added the chain later, gently
drawing my eye down, placed
quietly, answer perhaps,
after I saw and spoke
her delicate adorn.

Black heels in my hall, high, canted, strapped,
unfilled, waiting her foot, ready to move,
those shoes. I see her walk now, all lilt,
and breathe deeply. She looks back
cross her shoulder, hair bouncing,
lips half-parted, catches my eye,
swings her hips, cat-walking,
and dissolves.

A lone
borrowed book rests
on my shelf
waiting.

Will she come
to claim

what is
hers?

upright

the knabe spinet, untuned
brass casters denting wool carpet
gathering dust on Ocean Ave
sound board cracked, action uneven

left in a truck for New Haven
first floor, two family on Whitney
where wedged into the dining room
it collected pale yellow books

of chopin, scarlatti, bartok
debussy, satie, and bach
two part inventions and three part
like the fiction of yellow books

all were paper, but some were green
or cream, bordered brown and maroon
but g. schirmer defined music
notation in my age six head

so every collection of scores
was pale yellow and said, "schirmer's"
although there was no apostrophe
and no possessive on the page.

i was inventing a concept
of music based on my father's
determined style of learning
the notes, the dynamics, the feel

but nothing rhythm related
which lead to highly elastic
interpretations of chopin's
nocturnes, and the children's corner

in which golliwog's cakewalk seemed
like an off-kilter rag 'o jazz

an illegitimate cousin
twice or three times removed from monk

who played, straight, no chaser, in mono
on the big-assed, five speaker high-fi
washing machine shaped wood unit
that backlit saturday parties

with saxophone playing novelists
psychedelic imbibing shrinks
cunard line traveling scholars
and horny red haired divorcees

who drank wildman beaujolais villages
from cheap wide lipped five ounce glasses
leaving bruised lipstick on the rims
and threatened faculty wives

gossiping in the kitchen
as they plated brie and fois gras
on the squiggle formica dinette
where i refused to eat carrots

for which, in penance i sat
while my family disappeared
into activities unknown
except for my father who played

on the mister deutsch tuned spinet
with gusto loud enough to cover
the sound of me dumping carrots
deep in the trash, well out of sight.

Final Impression of a Dying Man

The clavicles massive,
Under sunken skin,
Moist, mottled, loose,
Depressing into space
Unmuscled.

The forehead, wide and discolored,
Reflects sorry grey light
From the un-faced window
Buena vista, if only you'd look.

Thoracic spine, crustacean curled,
Each vertebra distinct, popping back,
Exiting your body, organs dropping,
A pooling mass, splayed
Across immobile legs.

When I touch your back,
All I feel is bone and sadness.

When I touch your stubbled cheek,
I feel more: falling skin, not quite clammy,
Large, watered eyes rolling in their sockets,
Sucking breath, warm air on the release.

II

You know I have come to say goodbye.
We both know that you will wait to die,
Until I have returned to my place, not my home,
And that you will die alone,
In this place, not your home.

Funny that, you and I both misplaced,
And we know it, as I take you in, you
And your view.

III

You have steadfastly
Declined near seven years,
Making no concession to the place
Where you will end.

And so I rub your shoulders
And feel the wool of your worn
Sweater pill in my hands,

Your voice, distant and alert
As I draw your pain into my fingers,
Bounces through empty ribs.

It rises with questions,
Falls with answers
And flows with half remembered
Stories until the sun drops
And the room fills with storm grey.

You lift your head as I say goodbye,
Kissing you once on the cheek
And once on the forehead,
Rubbing back your limp white hair.

IV

I go clumsy to the door,
Smelling the dust of un-cleaned
Commercial carpet,
And turn in the crack,

Seeing bone and sadness
Merging into night,
Then a tooth and a smile,
A softening around the lips,
And that is all.

Paradise Drive

At summer solstice
The cars stopped on Paradise
Dropped their tops

And let the stuffing
From their tuck and rolls
Rise into the burning night

The radios
Tuned to the same station
Played loud

Bascom

In the dining room
of this old lodge

listening to the clank
of washing silver

and the rustle of the cook
steadily preparing for lunch.

Acknowledgements

I'm grateful to everyone who's read my poems, listened to my albums and come to my shows along the way. You've each helped to shape this book. I want to offer particular thanks to Gail Maclachlan who opened the door for me as a poet, and as a person. I've never known anyone with more pure grace.

I want also to thank Catherine Calvert and Lisa Francesca who read much of this work in its infancy, and the late Don Parker, my collaborator and accompanist, who taught me timing and how to listen deeply. I could feel him comping behind me as I edited this collection.

My warmest thanks to Holly Anderson, fine ally and fellow poet, who introduced me to Pelekinesis, and to Mark Givens for giving this collection a fine home. Doug Holder and Kythe Heller first published poems that appear in this collection, and Peg Simone turned my poem *Woodshed*, which can be read as a score, first into music and then into film. I'm grateful also to Sandra Miller, James McElhiney, Lean Sweeney, Archie Roberts, Charles Coe, Donna Creighton, Linda Aldrich, Jennifer Greer, Matthew D'Abate, Winthrop Burr, Brendyn Schneider, Aaron Shadwell, Carol Steinfeld, Erin Cressida Wilson, Caroline Garland, Claudia Gutwirth, Eric Edelman, Anne Fiero, Bob Holman, Gabrielle Senza, Colby Devitt, Jeff Haynes, John Lawson, Stephanie Berger, Nick Adamski, Arthur Nasson, Erica Ferencik, Julie Story, Rebekah Zhuraw, Deborah Oster Pannell, J.K. Fowler, Jon West-Bey, and Prudy Kohler, who've been friends, readers, critics, and champions along the way.

I want to offer particular thanks to Caroline Ratner, who helped me develop more set lists than I can count, in the process turning me into a much better poet and performer, and to Lisa Donnely who knows the secret of the Underwater Typewriter.

Thanks finally to Peter Barnes and the folks at Mesa Refuge, and to Peter Dudek, John Dudek and Brad Parsons at Bascom Lodge who gave me residencies that brought this work to life.

"*The Underwater Typewriter*—Bay Area poet Marc Zegans' optimistic and ambitious new collection…is a lyrical chronicle and how-to of salvaging valuables from the murk, honoring and saying goodbye to that which cannot be recovered whole, living well and meaningfully in spite of lost loves, youthful health, family mythologies and cultural innocence. It is also a mature perspective, as deliverable only by one who has lived long enough to know first-hand the pressure point of a manual keyboard or the satisfying clunk of a hard return.

Carol L. Skolnick, writer, Santa Cruz

"*The Underwater Typewriter* reminds us that the physical body is lost and helpless on the edge of mortality but that the soul will not give in, no matter what. Zegans is a master of the stolen moment; Lovers in different states of melancholy, reminiscent of Neruda's *The Captain's Verses*, the dangerous days of real hipsters fighting tyranny and spilling real blood, the forever onward push of the natural elements against man's languishing fragility. Through language and rhythm, he is able to capture these memories and images before they evaporate like smoke in a room. Or coffee steam up from a chipped mug. It is a collection of laments, but somewhere behind the voice of a wise sage with a really good pen, lurks the humor and optimism of a young man in spectator shoes who waits for these kinds of deep slashes to smarten him up. It makes you want to read poetry again. And to pay attention. And to live in one big gulp."

Nichole Dupont, writer, editor, fighter

"In *The Underwater Typewriter*, Marc Zegans uses a bracing surrealism as an edifying weapon, a strategy that unifies many disparate themes into a cohesive and unifying performance. In the manner of Revardy or Appolinaire, these poems are deceptively intimate, as the narrator sits in his abstract webs, and with deft precision uses his language to shake the reader's preconceived notions. The best poetry always illuminates the hidden commerce between unseen things, but Zegans' work also has a constant emotional honesty that does not truck in obfuscation or ambiguity; it is a poetry that strives to reduce the misperceptions that arise every day between cultures, genders, geographies and families. From the shards he shows us a deeper focus, a deeper understanding of what it means to be a contemporary citizen of the world."

Keith Flynn, editor of the *Asheville Poetry Review* and author of *Colony Collapse Disorder*

Advance Praise for *The Underwater Typewriter*

"No clichés.... No subtle walks through the park sniffing daisies.... No bullshit... Marc shocks his subjects with electric intensity of remarkable descriptive imagery while diving deep into unfiltered waters, getting beneath the currents of human interactions to lock eyes with his subjects before fetching his underwater typewriter. Each poem through the 133 pages is tightly crafted with laser-light jolts of focus without compromise. Marc journeys unleashed through unchartered waters from East to West coasts with the hardened intimacy of a lover and a dreamer without remorse, able to reflect his natural gift of crafting a poem."

Brian Morrisey, editor, *Poesy Magazine*

"In *The Underwater Typewriter*, poet Marc Zegans plays the seductive merman, inviting us with the casual wave of a flipper to join him beneath the surface of the ordinary world, where treasures untold wait to be discovered in the shimmering waters. How fortunate we are to have a guide of such intelligence, courage and compassion."

Charles Coe, author of *All Sins Forgiven: Poems for My Parents*

"...spunky, sparky...a fractured, fragmented and spirited collision of image and energy."

Simon Warner, editor of *Howl For Now* and author of *Text and Drugs and Rock'n'Roll: The Beats and Rock Culture*

MARC ZEGANS is the author of the poetry collection *Pillow Talk* and two spoken word albums, *Marker and Parker* and *Night Work*. He comes to *The Underwater Typewriter* through the bayous and backwaters of American poetry, having been the Narragansett Beer Poet Laureate, and a Poetry Whore with the New York Poetry Brothel—which *Time Out New York* described as "New York's Sexiest Literary Event." Marc has performed everywhere from the Bowery Poetry Club to the American Poetry Museum. As an immersive theater producer, he created the Boston Center for the Arts' *CycSpecific "Speak-Easy"* and *Salon Poetique: A Gathering of the "Tossed Generation."* He also has been MC and co-producer of *The No Hipsters Rock 'n Roll Revue* and co-producer, with Karen Lee, of *Burlesque for Books*. Marc lives near the coast in Northern California.

CPSIA information can be obtained at www.ICGtesting.com
Printed in the USA
BVOW03s0836190516

448700BV00002B/8/P